READING SZYMBORSKA
IN A TIME OF PLAGUE

READING SZYMBORSKA IN A TIME OF PLAGUE

Joan Baranow

Brick Road Poetry Press
www.brickroadpoetrypress.com

Copyright © 2023 by Joan Baranow

Cover art: *Seated Woman in an Interior* by Thorvald Erichsen, 1931

Author photo: © 2023 David Watts

Library of Congress Number:
ISBN: 978-1-950739-10-3

Published by Brick Road Poetry Press
341 Lee Road 553
Phenix City, AL 36867
www.brickroadpoetrypress.com

Brick Road logo by Dwight New

ALL RIGHTS RESERVED
Printed in the United States of America

Table of Contents

I

Traveling in Tiger Rain..3
Viral Load..4
At Arm's Length...5
Measuring the Oak...6
Means of Survival...7
Shelter in Place, Sixth Week..8
Across the Barrier...9
Reading Szymborska in a Time of Plague...............11
My Son Says..12
Getting and Spending..13
Caudal Autotomy...14
These Days..15
Venturing Out...17
Archeology..18
Aftermath..19
Phase Two, Family Outing..20
Clearing the Square..21
Business as Usual on Zoom......................................22
Built-in Obsolescence..24
Oblique Intention...26
Spring, Despite...27

II

Summer Ghazals...31

III

First Woman...41
Advice from a Moth..43
Instructions...44
After Many Rains...45
Getting Up There...46

Lunar Territory..47
Orphic Ode..48
For Jane Kenyon...50
Elegy...51
Wreckage..52
Dear Penny...53
Ars Poetica...55
Visit to a Childhood Friend............................56
Procedure...58
A Stranger's Comfort.......................................60
Morning Rituals..61
Elegy for the Family Cat.................................62
Playground Accident..63
Inheritance...64
Family Photo...65
Semi-Precious..66
Anniversary Trip...67
Late Summer, Afternoon.................................69
Leave-taking...70
Prayer..71

I

*There were signs and signals,
even if they couldn't read them yet.*

Wisława Szymborska

Traveling in Tiger Rain

The world's out there, beyond the pretty curtain
bought on budget from World Market.
Through red-threaded poppies I can see
the oak outside leaning towards me,
midday light on clumps of new leaves.
The tree is faint, but real, unlike the print
hanging on my wall—Japanese rain
as straight lines aslant, striking
hay bales, umbrellas, cloaked figures
with faces turned away, a horse with rider
just ten steps from the village, and then
the sea beyond, where three fishing skiffs,
each with one wet man,
are caught in this imagined squall.
The street narrows at the first house,
its door open and lit. No one's running,
they know where they are.
Is it real? I'm there as much as here.

Viral Load

They like dark, wet places in the house
to hide in, dividing, crowding out
the prior tenants. Unasked,
they plaster over walls,
paste the rooms with stucco. O_2
wants to get out but can't push through
new sheetrock. Meanwhile, outside,
the flow of traffic slows, blood cells
en route to the heart sputter, the city
lights blink out until the whole
power plant shuts down. Auxiliary
generators brought in aren't enough.
What's left isn't a metaphor. It's us.

At Arm's Length

Like walking into the kitchen to find
Ingmar the iguana curled on the burner
unfold his legs and ricochet
against the wall. *Smack*. Falling
to the floor. It's your job
to soothe him, his owners gone
for the week and you can't even
keep the matches away. He's got
some bad-looking splotches of char.
You remember other babysitting fails,
chasing those farm kids upstairs
who just laughed, swinging a rat trap,
you springing it with a hairbrush,
finally letting them watch TV
till the parents' car lights appeared.
No wonder the prof on the promotion
committee could see right through you,
can't believe you take late papers.
It's payback. Who knew how much
the prison job would suit you,
cons in ill-fitting uniforms saying
"ma'am" to your face. It's always the guards
to steer clear of. Like a reflex.
You remember the inmate doing time
for armed robbery, a 7-Eleven,
who walked you back to the cell block
just to say he'd get the degree,
make good on it, he promised,
and he put his hand out
and you, of course, shook it.

Measuring the Oak

I lay a length of twine across the broadest
width of the trunk and balance on a root,
feeling around the tree
with twine gripped in my fingers,
pressing against the bark
so it sticks. I must look like a lover
hugging a very fat man. Like Frida and Diego,
late in his life, their second marriage,
when her sap and his could not disband
though they tried. My son studies them
and is fed up with Diego, can't understand
why he'd take so many women,
even Frida's sister, to bed with him.
Narcissists, he says, believe their lives
are more meaningful than others'.
They are also often depressed.
Nineteen years old, what he fears most
is mental illness, dissociation from the self.
Is there no reassurance, nothing
I can say to him? First,
measure the tree in inches, divide by pi,
then multiply by five if it's a red oak.
By this method the coast live
oak outside our kitchen door
is 142 years old. The bark is rough
against my cheek, smells faintly of coal.
I press in, as if for a blessing,
not ready to let go.

Means of Survival

The ants act like they've lost something.
They cross and recross the same plank
of wood, dipping their feelers
below deck, as if there they'd find
the dropped contact lens, that crumb
of bread, a misplaced egg.
They look bewildered, bereft,
like a mom whose kid went missing
at Food Mart, who felt those seconds
before finding him
one aisle over, holding a Snicker's bar,
to be the last of her life.
But the ants aren't frantic, are they?
They check each crack, climbing
over the garden hose, fallen leaves.
One comes back towards me
gripping an insect, holding it high
in front the way we carry a baby.
Only not that way—unlike us,
with our uncertainties
about virus loads, infection rates,
whether to touch door knobs,
canned goods, the mail, each other, our face,
the ant runs back to its nest
to eat this flimsy carapace.

Shelter in Place, Sixth Week

But humans still make plenty of racket.

Road crews are at it,
chewing up asphalt, laying drains.

The neighbor, who's usually so quiet,
shouts at her son,
"Don't touch that again!"

Just this morning, ambulance sirens, twice.

Kids skid down the street
on outgrown scooters
just to get out of the house.

Out on the porch,
behind the fence,
as far as the curb,
we wonder aloud what's for lunch.

And then there's my son
who, still "in school,"
logs on for aural drills.

Until 8 pm,
when the whole town howls,
you'd never guess anything was amiss.

Across the Barrier

Six days of protests in weather calm
enough to launch a rocket.

It lifts from its own fire
through a few clouds,
the camera in someone's hands unsteady
following the flame
as it passes maximum pressure
into a deeper blue, while

down here gravity keeps its grip
on rocks and rubber bullets,
ensures the shattered glass,
the arc of another shot.

Blood streams down, not up, pools
like spent fuel in the streets.

The people are trying to speak
but words go only so far
and raised hands are hard to see
through tear gas and smoke.

Yet—even so—across the barrier
a hand clasp
caught by a cell phone.

Brief as a synapse,
then lost
among the frayed nerves
where gravity holds
a man crawling to the curb

while, up there, released from earth,
those others
float like impossible swans
in self-protective suits.

Reading Szymborska in a Time of Plague

In this book of poems
two pages are mysteriously splotched,
pages 185 and 201,

where drops spread
across not the most profound lines
but not the most ordinary either,

as if she had thought
of something else
in that moment

between writing "the grass is green"
and "as is normal with grass."

Maybe she was interrupted
by a knock on her study door,
a step on the porch,
an unexpected call
when everyone had gone to bed—

a call that brought bad news,
a joyful announcement,
a difficult choice.

At that moment tears fell
on ink not yet dry,
leaving a faint stain
but keeping the words intact,

traces of whatever had happened
outside the room
of this bound book.

My Son Says

Humans are the least evolved,
coming so late to the planet. He's fixing
his own dinner—ramen, broth, sprigs
of arugula. I watch his deft hands
arrange components
in the frame of the bowl. Like
the titmouse nest that preceded us.
Chrysalis. Honeycomb. Sunflower
labyrinth of the puffer fish. Aesthetics
serve the lineaments of desire
and desire is the root of hunger
and do roots feel? Potato vines seek
aloft the taut string, hold themselves up
without muscle. Cells are the smallest
unit of consciousness, he says
and digs in like the wolfish dogs he loves,
plant life metabolized into his
particular body. A fly dives into the room,
works out its angles
with algebra my son says
he'll forget after the test, while
the fly makes elegant cosines,
understands where your hand will land
before you make a move.
What blunderous creatures we are,
holding cell phones to our heads,
unable to interpret our own pheromones.
He slurps the last forkful of noodles,
puts his bowl in the sink,
makes to go
so I have to call out the obvious—
Dearest, wash that dish.

Getting and Spending

So much time spent ordering online,
so much boxed up and sent back.

The kitchen floor has a stack
of stuff nearly blocking the door.

There's the dust-buster that never
kept its promise, there's the lunch box
bought for school then pushed
behind the breakfast bars.

Christmas gift tags that weren't packed away,
darts for a gun that vanished.

What to do with these three dice?
With stuffed toys, their fur still intact,
each of their names so easily recalled?

Must we keep a wind-up caterpillar?
This balsa sailboat no one ever liked?

Our closets fill as if to build
ramparts shored against unhappiness.

Tomorrow, we say, tomorrow,
we'll give away that bag of Legos,
that doll with the velvet dress.

But not the basket of embroidery floss
(no one embroiders in this house)
nor the hanging terrarium
with its dead twigs and plastic moss.

Caudal Autotomy

Even with their faces shrunk
to stamp-sized squares on a screen,
the professors are still afraid.
More afraid. He called for an increase
in pixels, she cautioned for less, and
later it was a matter of skirting
the poison oak. Drop a bucket
on a lizard clumsily
and all you get is a twitching
tail. I did that when a kid.
I thought I'd killed my lizard
until my mother taught me
caudal autotomy. Since then
I've seen how it works
in humans—it doesn't.
We need fairly everything we've got.
Which explains a lot.
Some prefer to keep their faces sheeted,
some go mute, some are still learning
how to insert words into space
even without the current pandemic.
Sure, I've sent a few emoji,
been caught by clickbait.
I've pretended to teach in a cloud.
Like you, I've had my share
of amputations. Still.
It's hard to unmute for the joke.
When the host leaves
and the silenced screens go dark,
one by one the families come
out to face the emptied streets and sky,
hearing the sirens go by,
singing from their balconies.

These Days

It's due dates and tin snips
    left in the rain,
  an air to the chill, sour

grass slumped over,
    trees sending mycorrhizal
  messages underground

like teenagers vibrating
    under their clothes,
  thirty-nine trillion microbes

at last count crawling through.
    It's pig brain cells
  brought back from the dead

despite the no confidence vote.
    You might as well get up,
  velcro your shoes, the moon

is gibbous, which means
    big ass falling backwards
  or at least that's what it said

on the test. The cats are glad
    to lay their soft slab
  across your chest, even though

you feed them only dry food.
    Love can be close up
  like sirens in the middle of the day,

sandwich at your mouth,
    or jump in a spooky way
  across time zones, 3 am here, 5 there,

which means he's still asleep, the coffee
    not brewed, the dog's leash slack,
  the woman he loves a warm wedge

in his bed. We make our own beds
    though most of life comes at you
  while scrambling eggs in the pan,

trying to remember the last thing
    your mother said on the phone
  alone in the swollen room

before she lay down for good.

Venturing Out

At the bottom of the brick stairs
a baby rat hunched against the step,
his black eye-bead on me,
his tail pink and squat,
his pelt clean-looking, sleek.
He seemed out of place here
where we roam in family packs
doing what humans do—
jogging, dropping cell phones,
parallel parking
with awkward results.
I felt friendly towards him,
could almost pick him up,
which was weird, since I'd killed
so many in my life, happy
to release the snapped trap
and bag the body.
Me, a nice blonde, friend to all.
Oh well,
I went through the gate
and when I got back
he'd concealed himself
somewhere, shivering, no doubt,
counting his blesséd luck.

Archeology

First a sideways look
from female hieroglyphs
because researchers on their
dusty knees said so. Years
reproducing her voice and still
they can't get the chords right,
insisting on safety & peace, *as if.*
Then the women rose up
with their nailed shut concepts
about Nature, et. al.
They carried crushed icons
into the streets. Consequently,
the economy was pleased.
Economy smiled upon them,
said, Come into my mansion.
Down the cinder block halls
hung with clogged clocks,
I mean, blocked cubes
and not in an Egyptian kind of way.
Not like a cave where at least
you can lick the walls. Instead,
it's FaceTime, creased collars,
CrossFit & content marketing.
Women are glad
to have their time punched
under the orchid banner
that's tattered & torn.
Yet the wet laundry gets hung.
Some babies get born.

Aftermath

There's no funeral for the death
of an idea
no matter how loved,

or for the loss
of something made
and discarded—
a kid's painting,
a knit hat,
an academic program.

Every day something fine
goes missing, is tossed
like used tissue
or torn underwear
with no ritual for remembrance.

Just today news of another
death came over Zoom,
from one whose face on the screen

was clearly in another room,
perhaps at a higher altitude,
where decisions like these

form at lifeless elevations
and fall as hail.

Phase Two, Family Outing

We headed to Point Reyes
where the young families of Marin
were out with their dogs. Some gathered
in restaurants, their masks tucked
under their plates so as to eat
and talk without bother. Others
browsed in newly opened shops,
we among them,
touching the tourist junk,
breathing the air, oblivious.
Like a bad scam the virus
reinvents itself,
crossing state lines, appearing
suddenly in a shopping mall,
ready to infect. After so long
we've grown used to its threats,
like an ex you can't imagine
really showing up with a gun.
Not until the door opens.
And not even then.

Clearing the Square

The skull cracks on concrete
when shoved backwards to the street.
Armed men in riot gear keep marching
despite the blood flowing fast from his ear
and calls for an ambulance.

One officer pauses to look back,
seized by shame or conscience,
like Lot's wife who fled her city
where her people had risen up
against the authorities.
She was hurried uphill,
her husband's hand hard on her arm.

When she turned, when she saw her city
a pile of ash and smoke,
her heart broke.
And then the Lord smote her.

Better a pillar of salt, I say,
than to be this man who shrugs, and turns away.

Business as Usual on Zoom

Even as shrunken heads we humans
carry on the same as before.

You'd think being a postage stamp,
a bite-sized saltine on the screen,

we'd comport ourselves more
cautiously, aware
that the host can mute us at will,
neglect to invite us into the grid.

But we're still the same,
maybe more so,
since here's Jim showing off
his Maine Coon cat,
while over there, third from left,
Kate's rescue dog jumps into her lap.

Here come the toddlers
who need to know what's going on.
They push in
till their faces fill the screen.

Surely when the video goes blank,
our colleague hasn't disappeared—
she's just eating lunch.

So when the VP claims
the college can't sustain
its hundred-year-old music program,

does it seem a small thing
put into a little frame?

Do grief and disbelief
sound tinny through our mics?

Whatever noise our protests make,
when the time allotted
to this agenda item has elapsed,
the meeting ends with a click.

Built-in Obsolescence

The idea inside an image tries to shout
               from concrete. Each
    leaf hides an oakworm

the titmice find. Each
               atom wrapped in electrons holds an
    explosion.

Packages were folded in paper bags and tied
               in twine before
    machinery changed.

Beep, beep, beep, beep go the groceries
               when once was *ka-ching*.
    Now radiation

where once was surgery. We've all
               been there, or will be,
    supine on the table,

waiting
               for the gowned technician to press
    Start. Too late

for my mother who took
               one big blast.
    Easy enough, the tumor thought,

growing another
               path to her heart. Squeeze
    a baggie of blood and watch

it balloon. Balloons are useful
            when inserting a stent
    or making goofy

party hats. Even then,
            the membranes
    thin, vessels wear out,

the bagger is called for
            a clean-up on aisle 5. Meanwhile,
    the idea of sap

pulses. What you see in the scan
            are all these fat blue panicles
    of the jacaranda tree.

Oblique Intention

> *assemble some of the instruments in a group and treat the group*
> —Brian Eno, *Oblique Strategies*

It's taken no trail but time to get here.
Your sticky past falls back easily—
a sinkhole groping a whole house,
an IV sliding into skin
slicked with regret. He said,
Walk on the edge, and you do
despite the cracked asphalt.
There are others breathing hard,
upright, intent on existence.
They've given nicknames
to what's below, the better
to steer around marked hazards.
A circular stair takes you down.
Forget the fresh ensemble, the campfire,
its puny ring of ash. You thought
it would be lively in the chorus
of roots, instruments making
mute cuts in stacked stone. Stone
upon stone. Wet vessels tight
inside margins of bone.
Excavate with clank of knife,
tongs, tuning fork, spoon.
You'll need scalpel and suture,
a tin tray, rags, all those aspen
leaves slapping themselves,
an insistent finch baring its throat.

Spring, Despite

After our neighbor's coastal oaks collapsed,
our own felt the sun again.

Their long limbs, splotched with lichen
grew new stems.

Even the 100-year-old oak by the kitchen door,
its spine bent and twisted,

sent, somehow,
a sprout from its arthritic back.

Looking at it from within my own soft casing,
I imagine the pressure

as it burst its bark,
feel the bough suck sap from its veins.

Quarantined by the nation's state,
I can't help but check each day

on this late life birth,
this thorny bouquet.

II

*When I pronounce the word Future,
the first syllable already belongs to the
past.*

Wisława Szymborska

Summer Ghazals

1

A squirrel pulls a plum from the tree, takes two bites, then drops it
like a boy who leaves dinner on his plate and has never been
    nagged.

Meanwhile the squirrel's curved nails hold onto limbs that flail in
    the wind,
the tree dips back and sideways, weak in the knees. Little no count

plums not worth a penny, but from this window the tree
    looks pretty in spring,
dressed in blossoms. How a frame makes everything

seem sublime—cable TV wires, solar panels, the new neon
    tangerine-painted hydrant nozzle.
This wooden frame hides a spider behind a mess of cobwebs,

a dry mayfly plastered to the glass, one wing missing – a
    surrealist's view
of …what? The wind shudders a bay laurel, leaves the privet alone.

And you, Joan, think of all the dead deep in the ground,
gravesites rimmed with stone, the sated maggots too full
    for words.

2

I walk in as he's trying on the hernia girdle and hover at the door—
white padding and straps and buckles that won't cinch just right.

This man I've known since before our parents died—
my mother saying, "At least I don't have a row of pill bottles on
 the sill"—

puts on the age-appropriate garments, hearing aids, progressives,
with disdainful impatience, these insults he can hardly put up with,

his anger like the Father's wrath when Adam admitted his
 weakness.
Death would come next, ruining the life plan He'd imagined for
 them.

Sometimes I imagine all the work it took to tame the garden
 hedges,
Eve and Adam wielding clippers, all that rooting and flowering,

no season to let the weeds sleep. It helps to think of death like
 that—
a meadow muffled with snow, the tips of wet brown reeds
 blowing.

Now and then a cardinal darts across the white expanse into an
 icy thicket.
You've never been afraid of the cold, Joan. Remember that.

3

The crew comes back with its clumsy trucks that hum and grunt,
opening the road, trying to get the drainage job done

before the virus has finished making its own
noise, the sound of someone chewing behind a raised hand

to cover the tongue smacking as it digs in.
Like little pills off a sweater, with barbed velcro

hooks, they fill the lungs with lint, gumming up the works.
And now here's the turn

you've been told a poem needs, Joan, so that it breathes,
a swerve from pain—

The crew comes back on shift, masked, nearly rested.
One clips on an oxygen sensor, taps the IV line.

A patient, no longer struggling, is wheeled away.
Another sits up, accepts the bent straw between his lips.

4

The sun doesn't touch the earth all at once. We need doses of
    dark more or less
in equal parts to light. Which is why at night the roaches roam
    the kitchen floor

for crumbs and whatever muck we carry in—bacteria from the
    grocery store, pathogens
from the bank, office bugs, Uber germs, despite a six-foot social
    distance

and hand sanitizer at the door. We're covered with the stuff.
    300,000 years of evolution
yet 90% of us isn't. Better not to see inside your stomach. Better
    not to think

of mites hunkering down in your pores. At night they climb from
    canyons of skin
to mate along an eye-rim. After that they bust apart, spraying us
    with ick—or as this webpage puts it,

we were co-dependent from the start. Like fungus, hitched and
    cross-stitched, fused
with the flesh that feeds us, that feeds on us. Even so, Joan, from
    that wet dark

we swim into a world flooded with fluorescence,
not even bruised.

5

A towhee scuffs the dust where seed has fallen from the feeder,
its feathers puffed up like a dingy slipper, its wingtips dragging

in a maimed sort of way—a pretense
for the rat that runs out from the plumbago bush

and dashes back, uncertain how to attack. Yet the bird stays grounded,
making loud *chip, chip* sounds, like *help, I'm afraid,* or

try to get me you ground-grubber wingless thing,
distracting him from a hidden nest. Or so I suppose.

Once more the rat advances, then leaps back into the bush.
It's then a second towhee lights on an oak branch. Together

the two fly up into the air where they flit and frolic. Or so it seems.
This is the part that puzzles you, Joan, the meaning.

Like your mother's notes when she was dying, pressed hard in the cheap spiral book
she kept for herself—WHY AM I HERE?

6

I've seen them a few times, inches underground, or stranded in
    the street
stopped dead, like a machine turned off for the night,

all angles and joints and pistons and head that swivels side to
    side—
a backhoe digging the pit that sinks it.

Once one lost its way into a batch of breaded chicken, and
    I tasted
the acrid turpentine of its thigh. Child of the Earth, Potato Bug,

its body a striped orange and black oversized soccer jersey,
    its reddish
head almost too heavy to lift, its whole self shiny as if oil-slicked,

often called the Jerusalem cricket, though it's not a cricket, nor
    native
to that place, but the genus *stenopelmatus* of the species *fuscus*,

named for its narrow legs. Frightened, it can flip
onto its back, pretending death, then hoist itself over to burrow

and crouch, knees to chin, under a blanket of leaves.
Freakish enough to make you startle

in horror, Joan, remember? Lover of insects,
so you say, someday you, too, will lie alongside them

as they drum the earth with their bellies to bring a mate
that feels from afar those faint vibrations with its legs.

7

They must have been covered with fur, those first humans,
or else Eden was built at a Club Med address,

complete with gate and passcode to keep out stray
heathens who'd escaped their own dogmas

and come like beggars, barefoot, to stare through the fence.
Dark and glossy under the endless sun,

patches of hair rubbed off where they kissed,
Adam and Eve had little to do but taste

fruit at their fingertips. No music or art in Genesis,
just an abundance

of agriculture. And of course dominion over creation,
which requires sharp instruments

and explosions and projectiles to tamp down the resistance.
Cain flung a rock, then came the strangulation of the earth.

But this we all know, Joan, so what's your point?
It's time to quit this rehash. Remember

you were blessed
to hear Galway, with his hesitant speech, at the podium,
    reciting Keats.

III

As far as you've come
can't be undone.

Wisława Szymborska

First Woman

She took a shower first and combed her hair back from her tall
    forehead,
letting it fall in impossible kinks down her back.

She oiled her face and arms so the skin shone in the new sunlight
touching the earth, to honor the sun that may have been a god

or goddess or just a distant element bluing the sky.
She didn't know why but knew she felt the warmth

as she was supposed to, stepping barefoot from her shelter into
    the day,
as into a dream, the aroma of earth filling her with rich tasks
    ahead.

There would be tapestries hung for some and wheels carrying
    others
in a future season; for now she dug rows for seeds and watered
    them,

fruit and flowers for the body. There would be a man given to her,
nights clasped under a wayward moon. He didn't know why

but knew how to help bring forth fruit from her body and that
    together
they would make more lives and bury the dead.

They survived for a while and wondered without answers
or made up stories to amuse the hours

between the needful work. It was neither good nor bad,
or it was good and bad. It was one thing

done after another. It was before looking back on anything. It was all looking ahead.

Advice from a Moth

Never mind your freakish start,
your nine legs melting,
your face sloughed and tossed,
your skin like a damp slip
so tough to tug off, how then
for weeks you dried,
mummified.
Forget all that. You must
hoist yourself out of
the cracked pupa. Breathe
through spiracles that flank
your thorax like flutes. Cling
to a twig
while erecting your wings.
Dusted all over, crisped for flight,
enjoy the erratic path.
Touch leaf and grass
with your itchy proboscis. Veer
from bird call
no matter the song.
Your slumberous metamorphosis
prepared you
for loneliness. Be glad
those blind eyes on your back
never blink. On these brief days,
mating or laying eggs,
admire the silken city our species left
suspended in the trees.
Don't let light fool you.

Instructions

"Look at a very small object, look at its center."

It's a small garden. Late summer.
Nothing daydreams or dallies,
procrastinates, waits.

In midday heat cicadas rasp.
A dragonfly sweeps over the grass.

Everything here has something to do.

After Many Rains

I sit on a rock to watch
the tide crawl in. Cattails
already soft with seed,
green fennel high as my waist.
I zip my jacket against the wind
while a sparrow on a bay branch
tilts his head, quick
as flipping a switch,
parts the tiny scissors of his beak,
and pushes forth a frothy song.
He then hops, flies, dives
into brambles
of pale, freckled blackberry flowers.

Getting Up There

> *I rock high in the oak—*
>   —William Stafford

Climbing a tree
can't be easy
when you're fifty.

First of all,
there's no convenient
toe-hold

and the closest
branch won't bend
for just anyone.

You have to accept
scratches, pitch,
a bruised elbow,

skinned shins,
and whatever sight
the tree's height offers.

I imagine the poet
gentling the tree,
saying, "Whoa, Nelly,"

and the tree bowing,
early or late,
to bear his weight.

Lunar Territory

Being old never entered my mind, back
when, barefoot, I climbed the crabapple tree
and wedged myself in its forks, or later
tucked behind some guy's slick seat, his ride
roaring me home from the drunken firemen's
field days. Let me tell you it's weird to see
no one you know in the mirror, like, where
did that thunder back there come from? In front,
just wisps of my forest left. The whole frame's
askew, wobbly, like some kid's art project.
If lovers charted my body's contours
the way they used to (fair doves, the sea
of her eyes, Venus's lips, etc.),
they'd find a field full of snake grass,
a litter of cracked beer bottles, the dregs
of someone else's party strewn across
the ruts and hillocks of my hips, not one
hipster coffee shop in sight. Being old
feels the same as being young, only they
see you've passed into lunar territory,
desiccated, carbon-dated, tagged and laid
on cotton felt, a place they sense
but can't imagine, since
gravity's on their side, the trees more lush,
there's dancing on the patio where music,
drinks, and polyamorous kids compare
their beautiful new tattoos, where
sweet dappled apples small as walnuts
festoon the view.

Orphic Ode

I knew she would not disguise the gray
of her hair, as I would, that she would
stride through the famed city
with her young face framed in silver.
That was the one mark
death had placed on her, saying *not soon,
but someday,* while the rest of her body
kept its girlish curves.
And I thought how her mind could not help
but pronounce upon her physical self,
the flesh resilient, insisting on its mute,
ordinary life: feeding the baby at her breast.
Yet she would shake the tree of its history
and find her flesh either heavy
with stink or milky sweet.
It was her effort to know her significance,
her upshot, her once-and-for-all, her summation
and judgment at the gate
that kept inducing her labors,
forcing the words down
like holding a mirror to the ground.
Here is her muscular torso, her long feet,
spoon-shaped bulge of her cheeks, enough,
Enough, I say, her arms with their sparse, dark hairs,
bone of her breast the time I put my head there,
hard as a knob you could turn, and within,
her homeopathic heart
hidden from us, who are just her readers.
Her beauty, not bitter, but tasting
of the dank source, icy, black, trickling
through memory's uneven channels, like blood.
What would I say, if bidden?
Would I lay a plank across the mind-shaft mouth
and shout, come forth, accept your blessing?
Even where there is no light,

no rope, no warmth, no air, no square of sky,
I see her slamming her pick-axe into the coal.
I see the stacked earth opening.
I see the helpless diamonds
flying from her hands.

For Jane Kenyon

You would have liked how the early
sun lays a silver glaze
on each curved wrist of the spicebush,

and how beyond Stage Coach Road
a chainsaw shreds an old spruce,
its burr rising high...then low...
like strife followed by solace.

Donald's gone now six weeks.
We remember you nursed him
through his brief cancer, and then
the addled cells struck you next,
deliberate, as if with malice.

Nothing could keep you here,
not prayer, nor poison. You left us
the calm lattice of your words.

Now a freight train heaves itself
down in the ravine,
a cardinal dips past.
The cicadas keep up their steady rasp.

So much insistent life here,
the air sweats with it.
Life you saw into, the way poets do.

Elegy

Let this one be glad
for sweet pepperbush clad
by bees rubbed all over with pollen.
Let the tree-sized hum

be sung here in harmonies
though she be gone—
Sing instead words honeyed
as herself, a common mom,

mistakeful, wracked by rue,
yet fueled with insistent cheers
that salvaged all those years
for us, while her life flew

and fell like trillium
subsiding into winter's hush
under the longleaf pine—
Yet for her sake

let the rose tree speak,
let wild ginger show their sleek
white tongues, for once and ever—
Let mute flowers be glad forever.

Wreckage

for my mother

It must have come in a hurry
on a ship of pain, breaching
the weak sea wall of her lungs.
The tumor, split from its moorings, set adrift.
She must have felt that shudder
in her final minutes, listing as she ran
for her hospice papers—
all she had of a last command.
Captain of her body, she thought only
of us she'd carried
years before to this shore,
as her lungs flooded and she sank
down on that bed that settles all of us—
cold, dark, without human touch
and beyond recovery.

Dear Penny

Few of us knew you were Jewish
until we followed the pine box
downhill to the narrow grave,
your sons in yarmulkes and black jackets
despite the bright heat,
you moving easily now
aloft over the lumpy ground,
no need for extra oxygen,
just a light ride on your sons' shoulders
and when the rabbi called for back-up
your student Travis leapt to the task.
So many students there, sharing
their particular attachment.
Yet how little we knew you,
surprised by your world-
wide travel, your love of lobster
and bocce ball. You lived, your son said,
a *compartmentalized* life.
How can thirty years of daily discourse
and attentive, generous service
not be enough to know a friend by?
We pressed ourselves into the tent's shade,
appraised the soft Marin hills,
listened to the music of Aramaic,
then one by one laid roses on the coffin
as it hovered over the steep drop.
A hand-cranked winch lowered you down
and then we each slid a shovelful of dirt
onto your flower-strewn roof.
You would have cautioned Phil
not to overdo it
had you watched him reduce
that mound of dirt so vigorously,
but you weren't there to assuage us
with your unassuming care.

Afterwards, we formed a double line
through which your family flowed past us,
and now I think of you, Penny,
inside that box that still smells of fresh-cut pine,
the cool of evening adrift in your linen shift,
your crushed roses sweetening the soil.

Ars Poetica

> *To feel forever its soft fall and swell…*
> —John Keats, "Bright Star"

A freight train, fretful,
passing through the ditch,
complains of a stomach ache.

Its wail infantile, spasmodic,
reminds the poet to put
great spurts of static in her verse.

When lulled by a valvéd voice,
drugged by love, or opium,
rough it up—the sum

depends on syncopation, boist-
erous—steroidal—caesura-ic—
split signatures of tune

not unlike stomping a foot
to wake the student up.
How easy, else, to expire

there—pillowed on a breathing breast,
steadfast, starlit
mewing—like kittens soothed to sleep—

Visit to a Childhood Friend

We pick our way across the mucky yard
past a stack of rabbit hutches—
to sell or eat, she explains—
to the sticky kitchen door. Inside,
lit by a dangling bulb,
buckets of scummy liquid, flies,
counters covered with trash.
I try not to look when she points
through an open wall, just 2x4s,
to her daughter's room.
We go down a hall
carpeted by clothes—and it's
like walking on a person.
In the living room a crib overflows
with clothes, the couch where we perch
upholstered in clothes.
She says she never did learn to read,
can't even write a check but has to
pretend to fuss with the baby
while the store clerk writes it out.
She remembers when we were ten
I tried to teach her to spell *animal*.
She'd always loved animals.
Her yard had a huge willow, grapes,
a crab apple tree. Back then she taught me
to sprinkle each slice with salt.
She would toast white bread and sugar
in a pie iron set on the stove.
She says her brother did improper things
to her. She never forgot
the box of chocolates
the Malafronte boy gave me.
She looks around the room
stuffed with junk. She says
before the last home visit,

her neighbor helped dig out the house.
It took three days. She lifts her shoulders
and sighs, *Joanie, it just got away from me.*

Procedure

She lies on the table,
metal stirrups holding her feet
but she's not riding bareback,
not grabbing handfuls of mane.
Her hands are sweating.
Maybe she's been here before. Maybe not.
But the picture of a daisy field
is still tacked to the ceiling
so girl after girl can move her mind
away from the instruments and the noise
and the nurse who holds her mouth
in a way that could be construed
as any mood except the one
she was trained not to show—
the extreme shape of woe.
The girl's thinking about horses now
and how she'd like to ride across that field
of white and yellow flowers to the house
at the left edge where the paper has frayed.
She imagines herself alone—then not alone—
then alone again.
Alone is what she's been taught.
Alone is selfhood made holy.
Alone has no shame.
She doesn't even have to feed the horse
that seems content to carry her anywhere
within the fences of the photograph
that she can see has been ripped
from a calendar years ago
and taped above the table where she lies
clutching the paper cloth of this ritual—
ten minutes of pressure, muffled pain,
the nurse's hand holding her shoulder down,
the last limb picked from between
her clammy legs. Her friends are waiting

with hugs and soup and distraction.
Or maybe not. All she's knows for certain
is that the road outside the squat clinic
is covered in dust,
that the word goodbye has no voice,
that she will bleed,
that the horse will reach the fence
and step off onto the blank
expanse of punctured ceiling squares,
which is to say, nowhere.

A Stranger's Comfort

for David

You took the boy in your arms
because his mother had forgotten how
and softly stroked his sunburned back.
Everyone in the room knew
what had to be done,
his medicine dissolved in juice,
but you were the one who set the cup aside.
Sometimes you surprise me
with secret tenderness,
as when a stranger steadies my elbow on the stair.
The whole way home the round moon
silvered the lake.
I thought of the boy's wet face on your shirt,
his ear pressed to your chest,
his mother at the table, her forkful of food.

Morning Rituals

Brown Towhees are just birds—the same way most of us are just folks.
—William Leon Dawson, ornithologist

He names the birds that flock on the feeder each morning—
juncos, chickadees, towhees, an occasional jay
that can barely hold to the narrow tray and scatters
millet to the ground where the finches pick at it.
They make little symphonies, each bird
with its own repertoire learned in the nest
from its parents fussing over twigs and insects,
trilling or buzzing or whistling or making
percussive chips or melodies. Each week
he scoops fresh seed into the plastic tube
that hangs from the plum tree where squirrels—
when not plundering sunflower seeds—
grab the small globes, tear off the tart skin,
take three bites and let drop what's left.
He likes to watch from the kitchen,
his own breakfast of oats and milk lifted to his mouth,
before his cell phone rings, the computer pings,
and the day's demands brings him back
from his stewardship
of the common birds of the neighborhood.

Elegy for the Family Cat

There is where he lay, against our westward facing wall,
overheated, but still breathing,

from where I lifted him on his pillow and carried him indoors
to the kitchen, where we left him for a few hours

while we walked the city's tea garden. The cherry blossoms had
    passed,
the wisteria nearly lost its scent, but flamboyant koi enjoyed

nosing under the drum bridge for crumbs. We ordered tea and
    cookies
and sat under a pergola on wooden chairs, watching

starlings strut across the flagstone patio. Sometime then,
while we sipped from little cups, his heart stopped.

I found him where we'd left him, on his side as if asleep,
his fur still soft under my warm hand.

Playground Accident

When we found you in the ER
you sat at the edge of a vinyl chair,
stiff as a chiseled Egyptian,
your hands fisted on your knees,
your feet in their tennis shoes brushing the floor.
Even your gaze, so straight
I had to walk into it to be seen.
The blood had dried on your t-shirt,
so much as if your heart
had burst from your chest,
blood on your left shoulder where it had run
from the slit high above your eye.
You weren't crying but had the solemn look
of someone who had been or might soon again.
I hugged you, delicately,
and you let me without softening,
my son a stranger fully contained.
Someone had put a gauze pad to your forehead
and tied it with sterile cloth strips.
When I asked what had happened,
you showed me your strict dignity
and described it all—the lunge
and the fall and the metal stair—
with a voice
born of the calm you keep and bring forth
in the hour of your need.

Inheritance

There was so little left of my parents
by the time they died—
some cheap slacks,
three pairs of jeans, neatly patched,
cigarette ash, photo discs.
My father gave us nothing cherished,
his house already ransacked.
Just money to divide, that divided us.
My mother liked to live
in small spaces, her gift
of loving us gone awry, somewhat.
They tried.
We swept the trash
and kept what part of them
their wills had assigned.
Or was it fate.
Or was it chance.

Family Photo

The years between seem chalky
like the light in this old photo
blanching the background
of midwest trees, our shirt sleeves,
the smile on my mother's lifted face.
Time has erased us, erased
the park bench, the plastic doll
wrapped in checkered cloth,
my brother's black sailor cap,
even the cautious look my sister sends
to the eye behind the camera lens.
There's nothing left of this
despite our love
of legacy, things handed down
like jewelry, a talisman.
The past is gone, it's not a noun
or verb, not a stalled car,
not a locomotive on weedy tracks.
There are no tracks—only
this glance of light, an imprint,
these few words that clack
one after the other
after the other, and then,
not even that.

Semi-Precious

Hardware stores. Fallow fields.
Ordinary ballpoint pens.
Rain at night. Summer fans.
A tidy desk with plenty of blank paper.
Middle-aged Mauricio and Cesar
playing soccer on Sunday afternoon.
Bird calls I'd like to recognize.
Bright blankets on the beach,
each with its own radio.
Blizzards. Standing in them
with my hands over my face, laughing.
Laughing, especially at nothing.
Popcorn. Vanilla icing. Cheese.
Talking in the kitchen. Taking my time.
Decaf. Take-away cups.
Walking through fields. Sweat.
Rank odor of low tide.
Going barefoot. Paul Simon.
Cliff edges. Open windows. Iced tea.
Anything Italian. White socks and sneakers.
Distant hills.

Anniversary Trip

The cats come to the kitchen door
as we push in with our suitcases.
A week away, we are greeted
with suspicion and relief.

You unpack the food we brought back
into the fridge. Our son
lugs laundry in from the car.
I turn the furnace on
against the accumulated chill.

Everything is as it was
when we left. The dishes, rinsed,
remain on the drain board.
The freckled orchid is still erect.
Indifferent to our absence,
the house has kept
the water heater's blue flame
lit for no one.

Just last night we stood
on the highway berm
buffeted by rushing cars
to see the comet Neowise
flying from its dust
as toward an urgent appointment.

And then the space station
appeared—a burnished gold
globe falling in orbit.
Never again these together
here in the same sky.

You go up to our bed
while I look for what else
must be done. Tired by the trip
and another year gone,
I am grateful to the cats,
crying to be fed.

Late Summer, Afternoon

Wind hushes the pines
like the brush of your hand
stroking the cat
or like sand releasing ever
smaller particles to the strand,
breathy, murmurous, rustling,
as inside the limbic
louvers of your mind
where you keep thoughts of me
undressing, my cotton top tossed,
my bra a frothy dollop
exhaling its perfume.
Outside our room,
where we sleep in the spent
salts of our exhaustion,
late sunlight exhumes
from dust the scents
of paradise—rosehips
and coyote mint.

Leave-taking

Is the soul sad to see the body die,
unwilling to let go, like a sea creature
slow to unwrap its clasp?

Does the soul look back, gathering
its spirit as a girl gathers her skirt?

Does it watch with grief the skin
blanch, then blue, then stiffen?

Must the soul call to far parts of the body,
a mother bringing her children in?

Does she wait at the door as each one
runs home? Does the soul then

rise, remembering the flesh
as a bridal dress, laid in tissue and boxed,

never to be worn again?
Does the soul keen at this, or keep a stoic front?

Or does it disperse like breath
into the universe? Does it forget?

Prayer

Tonight a full moon lights the ridge
across the valley, where a cloud hovers.
The houses are dark at this late hour.

The outraged have gone home to sleep,
their placards laid by the door.

Let them sleep.

Let the grieving leave off their tears
for a brief space. Let the news
that breaks lie silent.

Let the guilty get a sleep's reprieve.
Let the judges and the mobs rest
together. Let the moth forego the flame,
the wound let go its pain.

Let quiet hours pass without a stir
while earth repairs.

Let dawn lean over us like a mother
reluctant to disturb, who must
lay a gentle hand upon us.

Acknowledgments

Many thanks to the publications in which the following poems first appeared:

The Banyan Review: "Archeology," "Leave-taking," and "These Days"
Ello: "Venturing Out"
The Gettysburg Review: "Oblique Intention"
JAMA: "Viral Load" under the title "Covid-19"
The Marin Poetry Center Anthology: "Lunar Territory" under the title "Being Old"
Nostos: "Advice from a Moth," "My Son Says," and "Orphic Ode"
Pulse–Voices from the Heart of Medicine: "Wreckage"
Spillway: "Procedure"
Women's Voices for Change: "For Jane Kenyon" under the title "For Jane"
Zyzzyva: "Caudal Autotomy" and "Inheritance"

I am deeply grateful to the Ensenada poets—Ann Pelletier, Judy Halebsky, Dawn McGuire, Claudia MonPere, and Barbara Tomash—for their support, friendship, and astute critiques. My appreciation also goes to the Community of Writers and the Virginia Center for the Creative Arts, where many of these poems were written.

About the Author

Joan Baranow is the author of six poetry collections. Her poems have appeared in *The Paris Review*, *The Gettysburg Review*, *Spillway*, *Blackbird*, *Poetry East*, *JAMA*, and elsewhere. A fellow of the Virginia Center for the Creative Arts and member of the Community of Writers, she founded and teaches in the Low-Residency MFA program in Creative Writing at Dominican University of CA. With her husband David Watts she produced the PBS documentary *Healing Words: Poetry & Medicine*. Her feature-length documentary, *The Time We Have*, presents an intimate portrait of a teenager facing terminal illness.

Our Mission

The mission of Brick Road Poetry Press is to publish and promote poetry that entertains, amuses, edifies, and surprises a wide audience of appreciative readers. We are not qualified to judge who deserves to be published, so we concentrate on publishing what we enjoy. Our preference is for poetry geared toward dramatizing the human experience in language rich with sensory image and metaphor, recognizing that poetry can be, at one and the same time, both familiar as the perspiration of daily labor and as outrageous as a carnival sideshow

Available from Brick Road Poetry Press

www.brickroadpoetrypress.com

All These Hungers by Rick Mulkey
Escape Envy by Ace Boggess
My Father Should Die in Winter by Barry Marks
The Return of the Naked Man by Robert Tremmel

Available from Brick Road Poetry Press

www.brickroadpoetrypress.com

The Word in Edgewise by Sean M. Conrey
Household Inventory by Connie Jordan Green
Practice by Richard M. Berlin
A Meal Like That by Albert Garcia
Cracker Sonnets by Amy Wright
Things Seen by Joseph Stanton
Battle Sleep by Shannon Tate Jonas
Lauren Bacall Shares a Limousine by Susan J. Erickson
Ambushing Water by Danielle Hanson
Having and Keeping by David Watts
Assisted Living by Erin Murphy
Credo by Steve McDonald
The Deer's Bandanna by David Oates
Creation Story by Steven Owen Shields
Touring the Shadow Factory by Gary Stein
American Mythology by Raphael Kosek
Waxing the Dents by Daniel Edward Moore
Speaking Parts by Beth Ruscio
Ultra Deep Field by Ace Boggess
Secret Formulas & Techniques of the Masters by Jackie Craven
Thrash by Michael Diebert
Face Cut Out For Locket by Jenn Blair
Natural Violence By Jennifer Brown
Miracle Strip by Matthew Layne
The Prisoners by Ace Boggess
Eulogy for an Imperfect Man by Maureen A. Sherbondy

Also Available from Brick Road Poetry Press

www.brickroadpoetrypress.com

Dancing on the Rim by Clela Reed
Possible Crocodiles by Barry Marks
Pain Diary by Joseph D. Reich
Otherness by M. Ayodele Heath
Drunken Robins by David Oates
Damnatio Memoriae by Michael Meyerhofer
Lotus Buffet by Rupert Fike
The Melancholy MBA by Richard Donnelly
Two-Star General by Grey Held
Chosen by Toni Thomas
Etch and Blur by Jamie Thomas
Water-Rites by Ann E. Michael
Bad Behavior by Michael Steffen
Tracing the Lines by Susanna Lang
Rising to the Rim by Carol Tyx
Treading Water with God by Veronica Badowski
Rich Man's Son by Ron Self
Just Drive by Robert Cooperman
The Alp at the End of My Street by Gary Leising

www.ingramcontent.com/pod-product-compliance
Lightning Source LLC
Chambersburg PA
CBHW021021090426
42738CB00007B/855